Let It Rain!

by Claire Daniel

HOUGHTON MIFFLIN

BOSTON

PHOTOGRAPHY CREDITS: Cover Veer. 1 Scott Markewitz/Getty Images. 2 Collage Photography/Veer. 3 © Masterfile Royalty Free Division. 4 Scott Markewitz/Getty Images. 5 Jeremy Walker/Getty Images. 6 HMCo./Shutterstock. 7 keith burdett/Alamy. 8 © Mike Theiss/Ultimate Chase/Corbis. 9 Paul Glendell/Alamy. 10 Jupiter Images/Comstock Images/Alamy.

Printed in China

ISBN-13: 978-0-547-02862-0
ISBN-10: 0-547-02862-8

11 12 13 14 0940 17 16 15 14
4500496268

Let it rain!
All living things need water.
Rain brings us the water
we need.

Plants need water to live.
Rain prevents plants from dying.
Animals need water to live, too.
Rain gives animals water
to drink.

There are many kinds of rain.
A gentle rain is a shower.
In a shower, a little rain falls
in a short time.
A hard rain is a downpour.
In a downpour, a lot of rain falls
in a short time.

Mist is a light rain.
The rain falls in such tiny drops
that you might not even see it.

A thunderstorm is very loud.
You hear the sound of thunder.
You also see flashes in the sky.
The wind blows very hard.
The wind may be equal to the
speed of a fast car.

In a thunderstorm, it often rains very hard.
Pounding drops of rain reach the ground.

A hurricane brings a lot of rain.
The wind blows hard
and trees bend to the ground.
Tree branches can break
and fall onto the ground.
People should beware of fallen
trees after a hurricane.

If it rains too much, there can be a flood.

In a flood, a lot of water covers the ground.

Floods can damage houses, cars, and plants.

But most of the time, rain is good for the Earth.
It is also good for plants, animals, and people.

Responding

✔ TARGET VOCABULARY **Word Builder**

A synonym is a word that means the same thing as another word. For example, the word same is a synonym for equal. Copy and complete the chart below.

Word	Synonym
Equal	Same
Prevent	?
?	Hurt

✏ Write About It

Text to Text Think of another book that you have read about a storm. Write a few sentences that tell about that storm. Use one or two words from the Word Builder.